To Derinda
I can feel your Spiritual
Light with love and Joy
forever

When The Spirit Moves

Talib/Benjamin Johnson 8th

authorHOUSE®

AuthorHouse™
1663 Liberty Drive, Suite 200
Bloomington, IN 47403
www.authorhouse.com
Phone: 1-800-839-8640

First published by AuthorHouse 12/4/2008

ISBN: 978-1-4343-9880-2 (sc)

*Printed in the United States of America
Bloomington, Indiana*

This book is printed on acid-free paper.

Dear Heavenly Father

In the name of my Lord and Savior, Jesus Christ, I really don't know where to start. Father, your kindness and mercy has me completely lost for words to express my gratitude. First of all, you have blessed me with good health and wisdom. More amazing than that, you have blessed me with the belief that you actually exist. More than that, you have blessed me with the humility to have faith in you. More than that, you have blessed me with the desire to turn my will over to your care. More than that, you have shared with me your Holy Spirit. More than that, you allow the Holy Spirit to guide me. More than that, your love is unconditional and everlasting. More than that, you are of all things that are great, and your abundance is evident in the compassion you have placed in my heart. For that, my Father, I will forever be grateful and aware of your Holiness. All I ask, my Father, is that you allow your Spirit to continue to cleanse my soul of Satan's temptations.

Please, Father, destroy the flesh that is so seduced by worldly possessions. Forgive me of my sins and have mercy on my soul Thank you,

Heavenly Father, I know with my limited understanding I don't deserve the blessings that you have bestowed upon me. So I ask you Father, in your most generous mercy, that you share with my loved ones or whomever you see fit the love, mercy, forgiveness, and compassion you so generously shared with me. In the name of Jesus and all praise to you Holy Father, your son, Benjamin Talib Johnson

Jesus & Brother Eugene

8th

Introduction

Dear Reader,

Thank you for choosing to join me on a journey through the most spiritual, emotional, and heartfelt experience of my life.

Thank you, Father, for you have blessed me with the strength, courage, and desire to serve you.

I remember thinking of my brother Eugene, and asking God to help me to endure the pain of his untimely death. I said to myself my brother did not die in vain.

I will give Jesus the credit he so richly deserves for aiding me in my time of need.

I'm sure that when you have read this short story, you will recognize the transformation of the souls involved in the process. The purpose is to uplift the name of Jesus and recognize the true majesty of God almighty. The other motivating factor is the process of mourning. I will attempt to show how, through prayer, faith, and spirituality, we can learn to rejoice in mourning.

I've realized during this most difficult time we can cultivate a spiritual relationship with our deceased loved ones. We can embrace our most cherished memories and allow them to sooth the pain of our lost.

God is most merciful and forgiving. The spiritual wisdom that God has blessed me with is truly remarkable. God has blessed me with a the most remarkable coping tool it is called faith". It can be shared with people of all walks of life. I have learned to embrace the reality of death, illness, and aging. Acceptance is the key to cope with reality. I hope this journey serves your spirit as well as it has served mine. Thank you

Talib 8th

This night was no different than any other night, until I received that call. The call came at 11:30 p.m. It was my daughter, Lisa. My daughter doesn't usually call me at this time of the night, but I was happy to hear from her. However, something was different.

The concern in the tone of her voice awakened my senses and set off an alarm deep in the pit of my stomach . I got the feeling that this wasn't going to be one of our usual daughter to daddy calls. She then informed me that one of my sisters had contacted her. She went on to tell me that my brother Eugene was in the hospital. She gave me as much information as she had, and told me to get in touch with my sister as soon as possible. I contacted my sister and asked about my brother's condition; she hesitated, and then informed me that he was in serious condition. She didn't offer me any details. She just said I would need to get to him as soon as possible.

She informed me that our brother was in the Kingston city hospital in upstate New York. I was residing in Seaford Delaware, at that time with my wife and her two biological children, with whom I'm raising as my own.

The news about my brother's illness triggered some old memories, and caused me to start reflecting on our past relationship, which caused a sudden sadness to come over me. I started feeling fear, anxiety, and experiencing racing thoughts. I have not talked to Eugene in a long time; I had no idea of where he was or how he was doing for some time now. In fact, the last time I had any contact with my brother, I was working in a correctional facility for the criminally insane.

It was a normal working day, I was monitoring the chow hall, and bang, it hit me like a ton of bricks. I looked, then I looked again, I got focused, and in disbelief, there he was my brother standing in the chow line as an inmate. The fear and embarrassment was overwhelming, I was afraid to approach him, but I had no choice. I finally dragged myself over to him, put on a fake smile and greeted him. I said Eugene, he looked at me for a moment, when he recognized who I was, he smiled and actually seemed glad to see me. We spoke for a little while. I never bothered to ask him how he got here, or what he did to get in here. I was only concerned with who might be watching, and what they knew about my brother. I began whispering to Eugene and trying to act as if he were just another inmate. It was a very akward situation for me. Due to the fact that I haven't seen Eugene in over three years. It was a very unpleasent surprise, due to the circumstances. How do I describe such over whelming emotions as the ones I am having at this moment? I wanted to crawl under a rock. However there was my brother Eugene, he was just the opposite. He smiled and greeted me like a true Brother should, with whom he have not seen for such a long time. Eugene was glad to see his little brother, and once again showing me unconditional love. While he was Standing in the chow line, you could see the joy, and pride in his eyes. He had this "Hey little brother, I'm proud of you look on his face." And there I was, standing in front of him full of fear, anxiety, and shame. The first thing that registered in my mind was, I had to somehow find a way to get him out of here. There was no way in the world I could protect him in a place like this, especially; being in another unit with no one having any knowledge of him being my brother. I knew all so well what went on in this place; these type of insitutions were violent, dehumanizing, and dangerous. But when I look back at that moment it was an opportunity that I allowed to slip away. I had no idea that, that moment would be the last time I would have to see my brother ever healthy again. I wasted that moment trying to protect my image. I went to the administration and requested that my brother be transferred.

I had no idea the next time I will get to see my brother would be years later in a hospital bed. Today, I wonder was I really looking out for his well being? or was it just good, old-fashioned shame. Coming to grips with that truth triggered deep feelings of shame and guilt. I can remember thinking back to when I was about three or four years old.

We lived in the Bronx when we were kids, in large a red brick house. I remember having an older brother who was in the army, a older sister, and an aunt who use to visit us from time to time. The two elderly people who also lived there, were our parents. Both of our parents at the time suddenly passed away. It wasn't until later on in life when I found out that I was left in the hospital by my biological mother, I realized that they were our first foster parents. I could remember on two different occasions having two coffins being displayed in the living room of our house with whom at the time were our parents lying in them. As a child they both looked as though they were just sleeping, and having all those strange people coming in and out of our home on those occasions was kind of exciting.

I had problems with asthma when I ws a child and on one occasion returning from the hospital, our father at that time grabbed Eugene and I from the back of our heads and forced us to kiss each other. Then he handed us a can of beer to sip on. It's strange the things

I remember at such a young age. I wasn't old enough to know how to tie my shoes, so I went to My Father who was asleep on the couch, so I thought, and I was trying to wake him up, I could remember pulling and tugging at his shirt, but for some reason he wouldn't move, or respond. Eventually my sister came in and tried to wake him up and couldn't. At that point all I could remember was being pushed to the side out of the way, and everybody screeming and crying. I never saw him again, until he was in that big wooden box sleeping, in the middle of our living room.

For as long as I could remember, Eugene was in my life, I always thought he was my biological brother. We had the same last name and were placed in foster care together; We were taken away from that family in one brief swoop. I can even remember the drive to upstate New York when we were kids. I could remember the family that we use to be a part of, and all of our siblings, with whom we never came in contact with again. Later on in life, we realized that we could not have been biological brothers after all, because Eugene was born in September and I was born in January, only four months part. When I think of the time when that reality became apparent that was another a huge let down. I realize then, and I'm sure Eugene did also, that we had no biological relatives. It just so happens that The Nixons had such a family oriented atmosphere the reality of not having real relatives wasn't as dis-heartning as one would suspect, we had a cool family. At one point and time in my life, Eugene represented my greatest source of strength and inspiration. Eugene seemed to have it altogether. I was never the type of person to look up to people, but when I look back on it, I have to admit I held a special place in my heart for Kirk. That was Eugene's nick name, I looked up to him and admired my brother's accomplishments at such a young age.

One night can define one of my proudest moments with my brother. Eugene and I were driving through town, dressed to kill. We were driving in a white sports car he had purchased approximately two months ago. Remember, this was in the seventies and he was a young black dude in upstate New York, in a small village called Ellenville. We drove past the neighborhood bar, where there were some friends standing out front. I was in the passenger seat, proud and cool as the other side of a pillow. Just then, we heard someone shout, "Yo! The brothers Johnson." You see, back in the day there was this R & B group that were called the Brothers Johnson. Can you imagine how cool that must have felt? That was one of the hottest groups out at that time. And there was my brother, good-looking, ambitious, and wheeling that bad ass sports car at the age of nineteen, cool Kirk.

That following morning I discussed the situation with my wife and made arrangements to drive to New York.

I began the trip early that morning, anticipating a long difficult journey. Little did I know the ride itself was going to be the least of my concerns. I started reflecting on the relationship I lost with my brother. The turmoil we experienced before he started losing his mind to schizophrenia, those thoughts created a lot of ill feelings in me. As I remember on this occasion;

I was hanging out, getting high all day, my brother Eugene was having a beef with some dudes over a female, and we got into an argument. To add to his frustrations, in a drunken rage I kicked open the door to this brand-new truck that he was test driving, and damaged the hinges. All my brother wanted was some support. I was too plastered, and selfish to be supportive or rational. I was a real jerk. I hurt him, and the look on his face said it all; it was as if he just gave up.

Our relationship was never the same after that. Not because we did not love each other; but because I went to jail soon after and never got the opportunity to make amends. When I got out of jail, I never went back to our hometown of Ellenville. I never got the chance to apologize. As time passed, both of our lives changed. Our relationship took on a completely different course: my addiction progressed, Eugene suffered with the mental illness, and our lives were altered forever. Growing up, Eugene always protected me from physical harm. In fact, when I was a kid, other kids would not mess with me because Eugene would jump in, and we would double-team them and kick their butts.

I can remember my sister calling me one day and asking me to come home and check on Eugene. I was living in Kingston, New York, at that time. I went to visit my brother, and while we were talking, Eugene began having paranoid thoughts. He was talking about government conspiracies toward him and assassinations being planned by the Goverment. I knew something was wrong, and the only thing I knew to do was to take him back to Kingston to live with me.

I tried to take care of him, but at the time, I was in active addiction. My life was very unstable, and I was struggling. I sold drugs, stole, hustled, and managed to hold down a job from time to time. I had a good job at the time as an evening cook in a nursing home. But the lure of the streets, and my addiction, was just too much for me to escape. I would watch my brother stand out in front of my house having audio and visual hallucinations, which was just too painful and embarrassing for me to deal with. When I scored marijuana, I shared it with Eugene; because that seemed to be the best way to relate to him. I am not promoting the use of drugs by any stretch of the imagination, however, due to our circumstances, that seemed to be the best way we had to relate to each other.

Eventually my life fell apart, and I had to move on. Due to my addiction, I could not take care of myself, nor my mentally ill brother.

That is a very painful thing to have to admit, and is still one of my deepest regrets. I abandoned my brother when he needed me the most, and those are the type of thoughts I am having while driving to New York to visit my Brother in the hospital who I haven't seen in years. In fact, I am thinking about my whole family. My foster parents had seven children of their own and took in five foster children. My father and mother were extraordinary people to say the least.

I finally reached my hometown, in Ellenville, where we grew up. As soon as I got into town, I went to visit my older sister, Phyllis who is wrorking as a preschool teacher. We were really tight, and she was happy to see me. We talked for a while and She informed me of what was going on and how I could get in contact with my other family members. I departed, and got in contact with some of my other family members. I went to the hospital, and located my brother's room. When I walked into the room, there was my brother, lying still, looking frail, and weak I could barely recognize him. He looked nothing like the Eugene I once knew. My other sister Debbie was already there. I could see the pain and sorrow on her face. She took me to the side and told me that she was informed by the nurse on duty that our brother might not make it through the night. This is so painful to remember at this moment that I am overwhelmed with emotions as I write.

Please Father, in the name of Jesus, help me get through this.

I turned my attention back to my brother. We made eye contact. He tried to speak, but I could just barely hear him. I just wanted to hold him, and tell him how much I missed him. Not only him, but also our lives together. I felt like Eugene was cheated, and that I was the one who deserved this fate not him. Quite frankly I was the bad seed of the family and the one most likely sibling to end up in this position. I sat on the side his bed, next to him and looked into his eyes. With a half-smile, I told him how much I've always looked up to him. I said to him, "You were always smarter and stronger than me." I was holding his soft, frail, thin hand while feeling humble and helpless. All I could do was stare into his eyes. He tried to force a smile, while he squeezed my hand, please Eugene get up, talk to me please, is what I was thinking at that moment. I tried to be strong, but I just couldn't contain my emotions any longer. I began crying hysterically; as my head fell on to his chest. I clutched his arms as I lay gently across his body, shaking and crying.

At that moment, I could feel all the reality of this tragedy, while waves of pain surged through my heart. My brother was dying, and I was helpless and feeling guilty. Eugene then made a movement to get my attention. With tears streaming down my face, my nose running, and being totally speechless. I looked up at him as he caught my attention, feeling sympathetic, and overwhelmed in this highly emotional moment. Eugene looked at me while mustering up all the strength that he could, and gestured with his hands, and in a very low voice said, "Get me some more ice."

Man, that was the moment, Almighty all-knowing Father allowed that pain to be mine and mine alone. God is so good and merciful. "I am thirsty, little brother, cry on your time. It was good to be here with my brother, even under these circumstances.

By this time, my other sisters and older brother showed up. That was perfect timing, and it was really good to see them. We hung out for a while. Eugene was getting tired and eventually fell asleep. We said our good-bye and left. I spent the night at my stepson's house; we stayed up most of the night catching up on old times. He told me that he thinks of me as his father and will always love me. That was a very kind and considerate thing to say.

That next morning, I went to a good friend's house to visit. I was planning to go back to the hospital a little later in the day. While at my friend's house he contacted a couple of old buddies of our's. We all met up at my friend's house and went crazy with joy when we got together. Man, Charles grabbed me and would not let me go he hugged me for a long time, it was good to see my old friends.

These guys were in active addiction with me, while Eugene was staying with me in Kingston. They were also good friends of my brothers. Over the years, we all got our lives together. Two of the guys became pastors, and one of them practiced Islam along with me. It was a great reunion. We reminisced about the good times, and the bad times. We were the Kingston, New York, thieves, and we were all suffering from the disease of addiction.

We shot dope, cocaine, drank alcohol, smoked marajuana, robbed, and stole; we were straight hoodlums. And due to the mercy of our heavenly Father, we all changed our lives and became productive members of society. We all have families and communities that we support.

I told the guys about my brother's condition.

They wanted to go see him. Although at that time I was loosely practicing Islam, I asked my two Christian brothers to pray with my brother Eugene. I never gave it much thought, about our different religious beliefs, although I practiced Islam. I knew Eugene grew up in the church, as did I. We all headed for the hospital to see Eugene. When my friends stepped into the room, it was amazing. I do not know how else to describe such a spiritually uplifting moment. OK, here goes. You should have seen the look on my brother's face; it lit up with happiness, and he had this sparkle in his eyes when he recognized who was there to visit with him.

I need a moment. I am crying as I am writing this part of the story, such a precious moment. I'm so overwhelmed with joy just thinking about that moment.

Eugene spoke in a clear, joyful voice, much improved from the day before, when the physician told my sister he might not make it through the night. The guys smiled, went over, hugged him, laughed, and started talking junk. Oh God, I cannot quite capture this incredible moment with words.

Jesus, thank you for such a precious moment, hallelujah.

Eugene was lying there so helpless and frail, but when he recognized our old friends he seemed so happy to see them. Looking up at his brother and our friends, he seemed so peaceful and content in that moment. At the time, Charles was an associate pastor. I asked him if he would prepare my brother to go home, to be with our Heavenly Father. Of course he said yes. He walked over to Eugene's bedside, reached out and took his hand. I was standing on the other side of the bed, and I took my brother's hand as well. Our friend Charles asked my brother if he knew Jesus, and in a low soft voice he answered yes. While I was looking into Eugene's face, in this moment he looked different. There was something special about him, he had this peaceful look in his eyes. I could see in that pain-stricken tired face of his, the beauty of God's spirit. Then, Brother Charles asked him to repeat after him,

"Eugene, do you accept Jesus Christ as your personal Lord and savior?"

To my surprise, with very little effort, Eugene repeated that statement, and asked Jesus to be his personal Lord and savior. I looked at Eugene, then at Charles; you had to be there. You should have seen my brother's eyes when he was repeating those beautiful words of prayer. Brother Charles began praying; you could see the faith in his eyes and the confidence he had in the Lord. My brother Eugene was dying from throat cancer. His face was thin, distorted, sad, painful, and had the look of helplessness.

But right there at that moment, with God's spirit in the air, you could see the glow, the love, and the joy in his heart. I have never witnessed a more tranquil moment in my life. My brother Eugene was beautiful while basking in the spirit of content. When I became fully aware of God's presence, I was overwhelmed with joy. I cried uncontrollably. I cannot explain why I was crying. Was it because of sympathy, remorse, or the joy of just knowing where my brother was headed. While the Tears streamed down my face I just knew Eugene was all right. He was going home; he was safe in God's glory. I have never seen or felt anything like that in my life. We all held hands, and the spirit of Christ flowed through all three of us. What a great, and secure feeling to behold. My brother was saved, and

I felt the Holy Spirit for the first time in my life; thank you, Jesus.

At this point and time, we just enjoyed the moment, the feeling in the room was comforting, and reassuring. I have always been a skeptical person when it comes to Christianity; I didn't trust in the traditional Christian faith. Well, at that moment, things started changing, the atmosphere in that room had awakened my spirit, and changed the way I thought about my concept of Jesus forever. I felt and heard Him loud and clear. Believe me when I say God had another soul to save that day, and it was mine. I responded with an open mind and heart, and ready for a change. Remember, at that time in my life I was not fully committed to any religion or faith in a higher power. When I look back, I realize that God was working on me, and I could no longer ignore His touch. That was a special moment for all of us. We had a great time in that room, basking in the spirit of the Lord. We laughed, reminisced, and glorified the unconditional love of God. It was unbelievable. I came to believe that Almighty God orchestrated the whole thing; it was too perfect, and everything fell into place. Eugene responded so well; he was beautiful, alert, and happy with a look of content that is forever sketched in the most significant memory of my life.

Thank you, Jesus.

Eugene began to tire, so we said our good-byes, made prayer, and left. That day I continued to visit with my friends and some other family members. In the early part of that evening, I got a call from my sister, it was bad news. She told me I'd better head back to the hospital. Eugene had taken a turn for the worst, and she felt I needed to be there. I reassembled the troops so to speak, and got in touch with my friends. My sister had a strong sense of urgency, so she started making phone calls to our family members and friends. I gave my friends an update, and they all agreed to meet at the hospital. That phone call was upsetting and scary, but not unexpected. I didn't know what to expect, except for Eugene to die. While rushing back to the hospital, that thought was the worst thing I could imagine. Although Eugene was blessed, and seemed prepared to go home to thy heavenly Father, there was still no way for me to be prepared to endure such a great lost. I'm dealing with so many feelings throughout this whole ordeal, it's absolutly mind boggling. In fact, at this point I didn't know how or what to feel. I made it back to the hospital and was approached by the nurse on duty. She took me aside and explained the situation. It seemed bleak, she informed me that my brother may not make it through the night. That was some very sad news. I couldn't help but to think why Eugene had to suffer his adult life the way he did. Having to deal with schizoprenia, homelessness, substance abuse, being unemployable, institutions and now dieing. It still feels so unfair.

At any other time, while feeling life was unfair and I was incapable of understanding, I would blame God and hold resentments against Him. My way of thinking has since changed, and I have learned through prayer and faith how to accept God's will at times and move on. This was not one of those times I was still in the process of receiving His glory, and had a long way to go. Well, in no time at all, my friends showed up, our family members showed up, and we had a special visit from a childhood friend and his wife, who became pastors. We were all assembled in my brother's hospital room, trying to look concerned and cheerful at the same time. Eugene was really struggling at this point and could just barely speak or move, his mouth was dry so I began feeding him ice chips, because that was the only thing he could manage to keep down. Both of my older sisters were there; we continue to have great relationships, and we were really close through out our childhood also. It was good seeing all of my family, even under these conditions. The atmosphere in that room was purely spiritual; there were pastors, believers, family, and old friends gathered in that room. A lot of love surrounded Eugene, and everyone was talking about God and Jesus. They were worshiping and rejoicing; it was wonderful. People were sharing some great testimonials, while disclosing the impact that God was having in their lives. They were talking about how their Lord and savior changed their lives. I was just standing to the side, observing and taking it all in. I don't know how to describe it, but the spiritual air in that room started getting thick. Man! The Holy Spirit swept through that room like a hurricane, and they started shouting and giving thanks to the Lord. It got so loud that we had to shut the door. Our Father brought all of us together at such a tragic moment, and he filled my brother's room with the Holy Spirit. We all prayed, gave thanks, hugged, laughed, and reminisced. Why was this happening in my life at this time, why is every moment so Spiritually connected? I was introduced to Christianity when I was a child, but I got away from the whole concept of Jesus as being the central figure of my spiritual life, because the image of Christ was Caucasian. Through out most of my recovery life, I practiced Islam. However, I wasn't really committed to following the princibles of the religion. I was not on top of my game and was living my own program, so I developed a spiritual belief system that rather strayed away from the basic philosophy of any type of traditional religion. I was still involved in Narcotics Anonymous (NA), and pretty much drew my spiritual connection from the twelve-step self-help groups. However, my involvement in the recovery process was so sporadic that it didn't have much of an impact on my spiritual life. My spiritual life was somewhat lacking, and I was primed for a spiritual intervention. This was no coincidence that my family and friends, who were all believers, surrounded me on this night. I mean, these people loved Christ and were not ashamed to show it. My brother had already accepted Christ as his personal Lord and savior. Now I think it was my turn. God was working on me, and by the time it was all said and done, I was wide open; in other words, I was feeling it.

Before I go on, I must make sure you understand that I believe whatever works for you is fine; this is just my experience.

As agnostic as I can be at times, I could not ignore the way I was feeling and the effect the spirit was having on me. I feel a strong sense of God's presence at this moment.

Please Father, in the name of Jesus, bless me with your Holy

Spirit. (This is what is going on in my mind and spirit while I am writing this portion of the story.)

Well Eugene made it through the night thank you

Father.

We all hugged, prayed, and said our good-byes; the impact of that night in that hospital room did something to me. I was feeling great, my brother was fine, and I have never felt this way in my life, *thank you, Holy Father and brother Jesus.* One of my friends invited me to church on Sunday morning, which was the following day. I accepted, although I had made plans to go back to Delaware first thing in the morning. I spent the night at a friend's house, and when I got up the following morning, I went back to the hospital to see my brother. When I arrived there was an old acquaintance of mine there visiting my brother. She allowed Eugene to stay at her house while we were dating. She told me that she visited him earlier that week, and he held her hand and would not let it go. Eugene developed a good relationship with Deveda, and he remembered how good she treated him. God, I missed Eugene, why did he have to get ill?

I remember when Eugene built this go-cart when we were all kids. He was the first guy on the block to put supermarket-cart wheels on the front and baby carriage wheels on the back, which made his cart the fastest on the block. In fact, when we were young, my brother did many things the rest of us kids could not do. He was very gifted with his hands. Eugene often worked with my father on the cars. He did carpentry work in and around the house, and he was just an all-around gifted kid.

That mental illness took what I believed at the time to be my only blood relative. We used to fight all the time, but he was my hero.

Now, here I stand, looking over my brother Eugene, lying in this hospital bed, dieing of cancer. While every fiber in my body, every thought and emotion I have; is telling me he does not deserve to live or die like this. There I was, soaked in the pain of reality, feeding my beautiful, dieing brother ice chips and vanilla pudding.

Life is about moments and how we choose to manage our moments. We are not guaranteed on the next one, so this moment is being managed by the Holy Spirit and the love that I have for my brother. Moments are either cherished, or wasted.

I told Eugene where I lived, and how far it was. I also told him I was married. I was not sure if he knew that or not. He seemed a little surprised about that. I let him know I had to go back to Delaware. I hugged him, looked into his eyes, and told him that I was sorry and that I always loved him. Before I get back to the story, I feel compelled to share with you my present state of being.

I am sitting on the front porch of a very good friends house name Reggie. It is a beautiful morning, and I just needed a friend to talk to. He belongs to the fellowship I attend. It's the year 2007 and it is my nineteenth anniversary of being in recovery. August 12, 1988, was the last time I used any mind- or mood-altering substances. My life has grown immensely over the years. I can not praise God enough or give the programs of Alcoholics Anonymous, and Narcotics Anonymous enough credit for competely changing my life.

All praises due to my loving Father who art in heaven. This is about Christ and my brother Eugene, not about me.

It was a beautiful Sunday morning. I left the hospital feeling grateful, and went to the church I was invited to. As I walked in the side door of the church, the first person I made eye contact with was my friend Charles. He prayed with Eugene and I at the hospital. As I looked around the church, I recognized a number of people whom I was familiar with, or once knew, which was a great feeling. I took my seat and started reflecting on the gift God bestowed upon my brother, and how I benefited from the Holy Spirit that was present in the hospital room.

I am trying so hard to put into words what I was really feeling in that room. I was completely overwhelmed with emotion and gratitude. It was as if I were in some sort of spiritual dream. I reflected on how everyone had gathered in the room and were sharing all that love and spirituality.

I was sitting there feeling so grateful to see my family members together for the first time in years. When I finally came back to reality, another one of my friends stood up and began his testimonial. I could tell that he was speaking from the heart. Because I could feel that spirit again. While I was listening, I could feel my emotions starting to rise, and I was getting this warm sensation throughout my body. I was caught up in the sincerity of his words. He was talking about Christ, and I found myself falling back into that spiritual dream. With in the moment, the church choir took over. Boy, I knew I was in church then. My body started moving; my insides started jumping, man; I was getting caught up! I was feeling all this joy, so I raised my head toward the ceiling to let God know just how much I really appreciated Him. I had this big smile on my face and I was rocking back and forth, like Stevie Wonder use to do.

Whew! I thought, What a glorious Father. Thank you Jesus, I love you so much.

Just as I was basking in those spiritual highs, I noticed they invited the children's choir up to do a number. There was this young girl, she could not have been no more than about nine years old. As she began to sing, her young, high-pitched beautiful voice sent shivers up my spine, and that was all she wrote. The Holy Spirit just took over. Man, I was going crazy on the inside of my body. I was tapping my feet, clapping, crying, laughing, and I could not sit still. I had this surge of spiritual energy come over me, and it was getting stronger and stronger. I was enjoying myself so much I could barely stand it. I could feel Eugene's spirit, and while I was thinking about him, I couldn't help but be grateful for the moment we experienced together with Jesus and our friends in the hospital room. When the music stopped, I settled down a bit, but I was really feeling it by then. I was wide open and ready to go.

I have to admit up until that point, I had never actually accepted Jesus Christ as my personal Lord and savior. Technically, I still haven't, but there was something different going on. Remember; at the time, I was practicing Islam, but I never really rejected the concept of Christ and the Holy Spirit. Due to the fact that I grew up in the church, I knew what was going on; and it was somewhat familiar.

At this time, another good friend of mine took to the pulpit and began reading from scripture. Then he started testifying, his head went back, and his eyes faced the ceiling as if he was searching for something. He started walking back and forth, and while he was speaking his voice was creating all kinds of feelings in my stomach. At this time, I was totally focused on his every word. He seemed like he was caught up in the spirit; he was really feeling it, and I was feeling it too. The message he was presenting, and the way he put it together, even the tone and sincerity of his voice, had me feeling things I have never felt before. What was happening to me, why was I feeling so ecstatic, and so emotional? This has been going on ever since I've been in New York, God it is hard putting into words what I'm really feeling. It felt like something was pulling me on the inside. I felt like jumping up, shouting, and running through the church. He kept right on preaching, and the louder he got, the deeper his words penetrated my soul. At one point, he seem to be losing control. Man, he looked like he was really enjoying himself. There was a moment where he seemed like he actually had to catch himself. It was like

I was connected to him for that moment. The thought of him almost being out of control, made me feel like I was a little out of control. The sight of such a stimulating display of faith, sent waves of spiritual energy throughout my body. I could barely contain myself. I laid my head back, and with tears in my eyes and in a soft whisper, I said,

"Please God, not now, not now."

Whew! I pray that you the reader can identify with what I'm going through. I became calm, drifting into deep thought, and somewhat bewildered. Can you just imagine what I was going through? Another pastor took the pulpit and began the official sermon; he was calm and reassuring, more informative then stimulating. I think that was just what I needed at the time. It gave me a moment to process my thoughts and feelings.

Can you imagine all this stuff happening to me in such a short period of time? It's only been a few days since I left Seaford, and my Spiritual life is going at a hunded miles per hour, it was all spiritual messages. Could it be coincidental ? What do you think ?

When the service was over, I talked to all my old friends who were present in the church, and thanked the guys who visited my brother at the hospital. I had a long trip ahead of me, and a lot to think about. I was on my way back to Delaware, but something was different going back. My whole mind-set was different. I felt alive and relieved that I had a chance to talk to my brother, and to pray with him for the first time since we were kids. When I was on my way to see my brother, I was beaten, I felt guilty and remorseful. On my way back after seeing my brother, I was grateful, hopeful, and uplifted.

When I got into recovery, I realized that I used to believe that God had abandoned me, and the cause of me having such a self destructive life style. Now I realize that it was just the opposite: God never abandoned me; He was with me all the while, and actually carrying me the whole time. Eugene was always there protecting me as well. Now, here I am, many years later, and God is still carrying me and Eugene is still protecting me, but not from physicl harm, from spiritual harm, even from his dieing bed.

Not to think selfishly about what happened, but I think it was my soul being saved on that trip, as well as my brother's. This time I could not ignore the signs. As I was granted the opportunity to reflect, and put it all together, there was only one answer, mercy Holy Spirit, and Chirst, Amen

When I finally got back to Seaford Delaware, after a long and gratifying trip, I felt great. I discussed the whole experience with my wife, and told her that it was a great trip. Although it was a tragic situation, I couldn't help but reflect on the spiritual connections throughout my encounters during the trip. I went to work that following morning and informed my employers of my brother's condition. They were generally concerned and supportive. I pretty much prayed throughout the day, I had a lot to be thankful for. I realize that my prayers were different now; they seem more intimate and personal. While I was at work I did some soul searching, I processed my feelings, and even shared what was going on with my clients.

Oh, did I tell you I am an addictions counselor? Oops! My bad. I make a living helping people. God blessed me with a special talent, the ability to help suffering addicts and misguided youth all praise due to Thy Holy Father.

While at work, I wrote a thank-you letter to the congregation of that church in Kingston. A couple of days went by, when I recieved some news from one of my sisters that Eugene was moved to another floor for closer observation. There was no progress in his condition; in fact, he was getting worse. I tried to prepare myself for the worst. I worked the evening shift at an outpatient addictions clinic and usually got off around 8:00 p.m. I was on my way home, but on this night I had an eerie feeling, I was a little anxious and depressed for no apparent reason. I went home but I just couldn't sit still. I tried talking about it with my wife, but the feeling just wouldn't go away. Finally, I got up and went out to get a movie. I went to the video store, but I couldn't find what I wanted. So, I went to the supermarket and found something there. I bought this old, black, seventies movie, a comedy; I figured I'd get something funny to lift my mood. When I got back home, my wife greeted me at the door. She had an unfamiliar look on her face.

She said, "I have to talk to you. Come and sit down." I went into the TV room and sat on the couch. My wife looked at me, hesitated for a moment, then held my hand, and said, "Your brother is no longer with us. He has passed away." I sat back, leaned my head on the back cushion of the couch, and closed my eyes. I could see Eugene in my mind, young, energetic, handsome, and smiling. Now that's the Eugene I really missed. Then my mind drifted to the hospital room, he's lying there, helpless, weak, and looking up at me. His eyes are sad, and distant. He was so precious and frail,

I see you, Eugene. I'm sorry. Why did I leave you? I'm so

sorry. Please God, why did he have to suffer?

I slowly got up from the couch. I headed for the kitchen with the thoughts of him standing in front of my house, talking to himself, no longer participating in life. Not being able to hold a rational conversation with me any longer or protect me anymore, all those years of needless suffering with that dreaded mental illness, stripped of all that God-given talent. And now, when it is all said and done, the reality of my brother's death. I began crying hysterically and called out my brother's name over and over.

God, please give me some answers.

I fell to my knees on the kitchen floor; the pain was so deep in the pit of my stomach it felt unbearable. I crawled on the floor, out of control with grief. I hollered over and over, "I can't move." Images of his life kept flashing through my mind like a short movie. The reality of this permanent lost punished my heart. It's like he is being snatched from my soul. My mind tried to hold on, but the reality kept pulling him away. I'm crying hysterically. I can't stop. I beg, "Please, please. But for what? To stop the pain? No! I deserve it. I left him all alone on the streets, and there's nothing I could do to bring him back. It's too late. "Please, please"; but there's nowhere to go. I have to endure this pain. I almost crawled under the kitchen table trying to escape the pain. I remain on my knees, my face pressed against the floor. Waves of pain came nonstop, and I felt completely helpless. But when it felt like I couldn't take it anymore *(God's mercy)* the calm came. It was quiet. I was tired, I remained on my knees, I was numb, with no thoughts, just feelings of sadness. I rose to my feet. I finally got my bearings together and slowly walked back to the TV room. What was so painful? Was it that; I had not seen my brother in years, and missed so much of his life? you never know how much a person means to you until that moment comes when you realize you have lost them forever. My wife was still sitting on the couch, with a look of deep sorrow and helplessness. Her face seemed to say, "I want to help you so bad, but I don't know what to do." I looked into her eyes and said, "This really hurts, honey, but I'll be fine. I can't believe he's gone. Everything is going to be all right Muzzy. I think I better call my sister and start making funeral arrangements." I got in touch with my older sister, and we made arrangements to get together when I get to New York. I talked to my wife about my relationship with Eugene, and how much I missed him. I don't even think my family ever realized the pain I went through while Eugene stayed with me in Kingston suffering from that mental illness. I talked about some of the good times we had. She looked at me and just smiled; she said she will be supportive of whatever I needed to do. I told her that I would dedicate the success of my life to Eugene, because it was through his suffering that opened the doors to the first time I actually felt the Holy Spirit.

The next morning I went to work as usual. My wife suggested that I call in, but for some reason I felt like going to work. I wanted to discuss what was going on with my employer. I think the best way to discuss taking time off is in person. I informed the people on my job of my brother's death; I also utilized my co-workers as a support network and shared some feelings with them. Everybody at the job was surprised I showed up for work, but for me, it was a blessing. I wrote the church a thank-you letter while I was on duty. That evening I spoke with my clients about death and using the coping mechanisms that I learned in the process of recovery. I obtained the coping skills and faith in a Higher Power To deal with tragedies like this without having to use drugs and alcohol to deal with the pain, and grief. It was a very productive session for me as well as my clients. I used my tragedy to help others learn how to deal with death. I also had a great opportunity to testify about the experience I had with Christ. When I told my group how God was working in my life, they were in awe. I could see the empathy and concern in their eyes. They were really focused and attentive. They were appreciative and grateful that I shared such sensitive information with them. My clients were also a bit surprised that I even showed up for work. Nevertheless, at that moment I started to understand just how insignificant I am in the big scheme of things, and God's plan is always the best of plans.

When I look back at all of the events that had taken place, and how my heavenly Father orchestrated such a spiritually enlightening journey, I can't help but grasp at the possibility of a truly divine intervention.

While I counseled the adolescents, I could see how God was working in their lives and using me as a vessel to deliver this message of hope and reality to them. It just so happens that my brother was a long-time marijuana abuser and cigarette smoker, which I believe was caused by his mental illness.

Eugene was just too ambitious and focused to allow a substance to ruin his destiney. In my professional opinion he was self medicating. Eugene was a shcizophrenic with limited resources, and no support system.

I showed my adolescent clients the real dangers of abusing marijuana by using my brother's death as an example. I admitted to them that my brother had just died of throat cancer, and his use of marijuana may have contributed to his illness. I do not know how much of an impact this had on them, but I wasn't going to pass up the opportunity to share this real-life tragedy that was most likely related to drug abuse. I enjoyed working with these kids, and it gave me a sense of accomplishment when they would share with me their undivided attention. Through most of the day, I wasn't as sad as one would expect. I was preoccupied with Christ and this strong a sense of well-being. Being at work was therapeutic for me. It allowed me to get out of myself and to focus on others.

Do you see how God was moving in my life at this time? Here's how I witnessed the power of God, these people were living in Maryland and had no idea of who Eugene was. However, through his death, they are receiving one of the most profound messages I have ever shared with them.

I vowed that my brother's death would not be in vain. Writing this short story was the only way I could think of that would allow me to honor my brother's life. But it was the Holy Spirit that inspired me to go through with, And it was God who gave me the courage to believe that I could write it. So I need not take any credit for the souls that may be touched by this message of hope. Its not just a story; it is a message. I am sure there are thousands of family members all over the world who have experienced the same type of spiritual intervention, and tragic circumstances. But I felt obligated to share the spiritual journey I experienced during this eye opening, life changing transformation.

That day turned out to be very productive and meaningful for my clients as well as for me. I felt different; I think I was walking in the Spirit. I don't know for sure what I was going through. All I know is that it felt good.

It was time for me to get off work go home and prepare to go back to New York. I was informed that all the funeral arrangements were made, and all I had to do was show up. My wife decided to go with me, which will turn out to be another blessing.

Most of my family met upstate at my niece Kim's house; she put together a barbecue for the family and friends. When we got there, everyone was pleasant and excited to see my wife and I, especially my sisters. They really liked Muzette; over the years, they have developed a strong bond with her, and they all showed up at the cookout. I've always had good relationships with my sisters. Although this was a time for mourning, we really enjoyed each other's company and made the best out of a rough situation. We had a great time at the cookout, we caught up with old times, and shared what was going on in our lives now.

Sadly, one of our other brothers has been missing for some time now, and even after six years, he is still missing. We talked about that also. No one in our family has been able to contact him. His name is Preston Nixon, his last known where abouts were in Florida. That is a very sore topic also, because we don't have any answers. While mourning the death of Eugene, we could not help but focus on the disappearance of Preston.

We mingled and managed to have a very pleasant time throughout the day, thank you, Lord. The day went almost perfect. In fact, there was an NBA playoff basketball game on, and my favorite team was playing. Do you want to hear something crazy? I was watching the Lakers; they were down with a few seconds left on the clock. The ball came off the rim, and the other team tapped it out to mid-court. Robert Horry caught it and threw it up for a three-pointer that won the game. That was a happy moment for me; man, did I give those player haters the business after that. When the night finally ended, we said our good-byes and stopped for the day. Man, we had a really good time. We were on the way to my sister's house when we received the news that my brother's funeral was pushed back another day. That was fine by me; it gave me another day to visit with friends and family. I live so far away I do not get many opportunities to visit with my friends and family, so this was a blessing.

During this period of time, things seemed just a little different, I felt calm, grateful, and in control. My spirit was high, and I felt helpful and supportive of my family. At one point and time in my life, I was the reckless little brother that didn't care about nothing but the street life. However, things have changed over the years. My beautiful sisters actually look up to me now.

God, I am so grateful for recovery and surrendering to the Holy Spirit.

I am starting to realize that due to this recovery process and faith in a higher power, my family views me as an entirely different person. I am now someone that can be supportive and trustworthy.

The next day we hung out, and Kim sparked up another barbecue, we gathered together and just enjoyed each other's company. Well, it was Tuesday night and the funeral was tomorrow. I had a feeling I was not going to get much sleep, so I went to my source of strength. I prayed and asked God to please calm me down and allow me to get some rest; I managed to get a sufficient amount of sleep. I got up early that morning, before anyone else in the house. While I was sitting at the kitchen table processing my thoughts, my little sister Lisa walked in. We always had a special relationship, so just seeing her brought joy to my heart. I named my first daughter after her, well; actually my girlfriend named my daughter after my sister; she knew how close we were. We started talking about family matters and the upcoming funeral. Lisa began telling me the way she felt about our relationship through out most of her life. She told me how much she always looked up to me, and that all she wanted was my approval and love. She then started crying (unbelievable). It was such a heartfelt moment that tears welled up in my eyes, I gave her a great big hug and told her that she was always my precious little sister. It is hard to believe the moments I been having during this journey.

This is all real stuff, and God is feeding it into my memory as clear as crystal. Then she began to reminisce about Eugene. She talked about how smart he was, and how she admired him. I was in one hundred percent agreement. She asked me if I was going to speak at my brother's homecoming. I told her that the family had already arranged it.

I have to stop writing at this moment to thank my Lord and savior Jesus, because it just hit me like a ton of bricks how much my family really loves me. I was once an out-of-control, drug-addicted criminal and street thug. If you only knew just how far Almighty God has brought me, you could identify just how overwhelmed I am at this very moment. I'm very emotional and crying as I am realizing the Glory of thy Father. I am still full of His Spirit to this very day, and it is real.

Please bear with me for a moment. I really need to pray.

(Dear Father, in the name of Jesus, thank you so much for giving me the opportunity

to praise you. Father, thank you for blessing me with your precious Spirit. Please Father, guide my hands, and allow me to share your message with those to whom you will, that I may worship you and submit to your will and not mine. Thank you Father, in the name of Jesus, Amen.)

I realize how unorthodox it must be to stop in the middle of writing and put in a personal prayer. However there is never a wrong time to Glorify His name, I have to go with the Spirit; the whole purpose of living is to please God. When I feel that I am doing what is pleasant to my Father, my self-worth is raised. There was a time in my life when I would never have publicly confessed my love for God.

My wife had not awakened yet, so my sister and I decided to go into town. That was a good visit and a great conversation; we picked up some breakfast food and headed back to the house. I hung around for a little while, then told my wife that I wanted to go to the mountain and pray. For some reason, I just felt like being alone, to talk to God.

I was on my way up to the mountain and was about to cross this little bridge when I remembered this was where Eugene and I used to go swimming. When I looked over at the spot, there was a no trespassing sign blocking the entrance to the path that lead us to where we use to play. Something told me I didn't have to go any further. My brother and I, along with our childhood friends, used to play and swim at the base of this mountain. I parked my car across the street and walked over to the path by the south side of the bridge. There was a chain blocking the path; I stepped over the chain on to the path. There were thick trees on both sides, that leaned over and almost touched at the top above my head, I could barely see the sun peeking through the leaves. It was about eighty degrees that day, but under those trees, it must have been about seventy degrees; it was like a natural air-conditioning in there. There was this beautiful waterfall coming down off the mountain, along with this cool breeze, and this clean fresh smell in the air. A small waterfall ran over these smooth rocks and emptied into this small body of water that looked like an elephant's foot. We used to swim in there when we were kids. I can imagine all of us in there right now. What a wonderful moment. It felt so good being there; it was like the good old days. We use to play, swim, piss, and drink out of the pond under the same stream of water yuk! Everything is so quiet, the only sounds that I could hear were the chirping of birds, the sound of the waterfall, and the crunching of the leaves under my feet; it was like pure paradise.

I lifted my head and looked up into the sky, with the sun just barely peeking through a mass of leaves. I paused, and inhaled in all of this precious moment, but something was missing, I needed something more. My mind was wandering, and finally for the first time in my life,

I spoke directly to Jesus, and said to Him, "Jesus, I heard that if I asked You, You would help me, so I'm asking you, please help me. Jesus, will You be my personal Lord and Savior?"

I paused for a moment, still facing towards the sky with my eyes closed. I was waitng for some sort of sign letting me know that he heard me. It was silent, I had no thoughts, no movements, just waiting for something to happen. I don't recall anything happening that I could put my finger on, however I felt calm; I was not anxious anymore. My thoughts were clear, so I just slowly strolled down the path toward the bridge.

When I got to my car, I suddenly realized I was running late for the funeral. When I got back to my sister's house, my wife was the only person still there. She was scurrying around and straightening up the house. She told me we were running late, and I had better get a move on. However, for some reason, I was so calm. In fact, I told my wife that everything was fine; we had plenty of time. I went to the bathroom to clean up. I looked in the mirror and began to reflect the special moment I just experienced at the stream. I smiled and thought to myself, He answered my prayer He's with me.

I got dressed, and off to the funeral we went. When we got to the church where the funeral was being held, there were so many familiar faces it felt like a reunion. I hung outside for a while, greeting my family members and friends, along with making introductions. I was feeling grateful and content, things just felt different, that is the only way I can explain it. It was as if these people were going to witness something special. My mood was, upbeat, and elated which might seem a bit strange when considering the circumstances.

This was a day of mourning, but it felt like something else. I went into the church, where most of my family members were already seated. I looked to the front of the church, and there was the coffin. I could see my brother's body. I reluctantly walked up to the front of the church and took one glance at my brother's body. I looked in his face and just walked away. That was enough; he looked so strange, I really could not see Eugene in that corpse. My wife and I walked over to the other side of the church and took our seats. I took her hand and told her how I felt about seeing my brother in that position. She said she understood. Just as we got situated, another good friend of mine came over and greeted us. We exchanged some pleasant conversation. I introduced him to my wife, and he then left and took a seat.

While I was sitting and reflecting, I glanced up front and saw my younger sister crying. I asked my wife to excuse me for a moment, so I could go talk to my sister. I went up front, sat by Lisa, and placed my arms around her shoulders to console her. She then asked me again, "Would you please say something for the family?" It was becoming more and more apparent that it was important that I represent the family.

When I was growing up, I may have been the most visible family member due to my outrageous antics, but I was never the most responsible or supportive member. Man, things have changed.

Being clean and having faith in a higher power makes a world of difference in how my siblings see me now. That is something that I am really proud of, and believe me, I am.

We hugged, while embracing the pain of our loss, and cried together. What can I say about these cherished moments? By this time, my whole family had assembled in the church.

There is something about the permanence of death that purifies the thoughts.

Most of time, I pretty much avoided looking up at our brother's body lying in that coffin. I was praying to myself and reflecting on the relationships I have with my family. I had all kinds of thoughts going on in my mind at this time. Well, the scene was set, and everyone was in place. The church ushers directed everyone to view the body before we got started with the services. I declined and remained in my seat; I did not see any need to view the body up close again, and it did not look like him anyway. The services finally got started. My older sister Phyllis took ill, and had to leave the church. My sister Phyllis, with whom I have a great relationship, suffers from a severe case of asthma. Phyllis was tight with Eugene and I while we were growing up, Boy; I was just thinking about the fun me and Phyllis use to have, upstairs in our house.

The pastor began the services by conducting an open prayer. This was such a special moment. The minister was one of our childhood friends. He talked about our friendships and the things we used to do when we were young.

Can you imagine how much of a blessing it is, just knowing that most of our childhood friends were doing well and walking a righteous path? This is a remarkable reality to behold, and here we were all gathered here in the sight of God. Celebrating our brother's home coming.

The two pastors facilitating the service used to play with us at   that stream I was praying at earlier this morning. One of the pastors began to address the church. He talked about not being religious but being Holy. He said, "I am a Holy Man." That drew all of my attention and respect. He talked about having a personal relationship with God. He also reflected on the relationship he had with Eugene, and my brother's unique character. He was very kind with his words—and truthful. My brother was a good person; I no longer questioned God's motives for the stuggles Eugene had to endure, because God is the best of planners, and all knowing. God orchestrated a great send-off for my brother. It was truly a blessing, thank you Jesus. The pastor asked if any of the family members wanted to say anything on behalf of the deceased. Our oldest brother still living, Bobby went up and offered a few words of encouragement to the family. He seemed a bit nervous, but very sincere.

On his way back to the seat, he gave me that look: "OK Benj, you're up." The whole time I sat there, I was preoccupied with the spirit of the church, and how the thought of Jesus being in my life impacted the way I was feeling. I felt different about this whole situation. I stood up to address the church with no thoughts in mind, just a feeling of gratitude. This was a great opportunity to express and witness the glory of Christ; I had never done that.

Just reflecting back at that moment sends chills through my body. remembering all my family members and friends present, at my brother's funeral, brings tears to my eyes while reflecting on the significance of that moment, so I'm going to pause for a moment to gain my composure. To be blessed with the ability to identify and feel my emotions is truly a gift. Again going back over these events are creating Spiritual connections.

Only God could orchestrate such a spiritually moving moment as this. He can assemble all these people in one place with all these spiritual, and emotional bonds. Only God can put a dope fiend with a history like mine in front of all these people to represent the Holy Spirit of Jesus, along with my beloved family.

I can actually feel the Holy Spirit right at this moment. Please Father, thank you so much Oh my God, I am so high right now, I love you so much.

I am not in the church now, I am at home in my room, feeling all these emotions six years later; is that amazing or what?

Well here I am, standing in front of my family, friends, and my deceased brother Eugene, while filled with the Holy Spirit. I pace back and forth, I look out over the congregation, and I look back and take a glance at my brother's body. I turn my attention back to the church, and there is my oldest sister Magary. I could see the look of approval on her beautiful face as she smiles at me. That says it all. I have so much to say, but where do I start. I see the pastor who conducted the prayer in the hospital room when Eugene made Jesus his personal Lord and savior. The look he had on his face when we made eye contact was as if he knew what I was feeling or going to say. With the look of anticipation on his face; he was smiling, his expression saying, "Come on brother, we're ready." I was calm now, the spirit was flowing, I knew God was with me, and my words would be inspired by the Holy Spirit. I cannot recall everything I said verbatim, but I do remember some key points. First, I looked at my family members and said everything is fine. I was not just saying that, I felt it. I reminded them, how through all the crap, the trials, and tribulations Eugene endured, he still remained morally grounded. I couldn't even make that claim, and I admitted it, in front of the whole congregation. My brother was mentally ill and did not do one-tenth of the insane crap that I had commited through out my life. Eugene never intentionally hurt anyone, and he had a moral barometer that kept him in line to receive the Holy Spirit.

I explained to the congregation how I would have given my right arm to be where Eugene is now, because I believed with all my heart that he would end up in paradise with the prophets and believers. The jury is still out on me, and I have to maintain obedience from here on out to get to where Eugene is already headed. Thank God! The fact that Eugene has passed away, leaves only two the truths to ponder. Accepting the truth is the only thing that allows us to get through the grieving process. I talked about how I believe God will grant all of us an opportunity, through our actions, to leave positive memories. In death, the only two truths to ponder are whether you were an example of what not to be or an example of what to be. Our family members and friends will remember these truths, and the actions of us all will dictate what the memories will hold.

Fortunately, Eugene left an example of what to be, which is truly a blessing, since he had so many obstacles in his path. I told the church that I believe in spiritual relationships and that he was looking down on us as we are gathered here on his behalf. I said not to mourn through shame, guilt, or pity, because he might feel our pain, but to rejoice in the homecoming. I told the church about the hospital visit alone with our friend Pastor Charles and how he delivered Eugene to Christ. I told them when I looked in Eugene's eyes I could see comfort and beauty. I said I could feel the Spirit of Christ in Eugene, and I knew he was safe. I said, "Rejoice, he is going home, church." I do not know what came over me, but at that point, I was not myself. Something happened when I started talking about Christ. I said, "We may miss him in the physical, but his spirit is with us right now." At that time, I told the church what happened to me at the stream that morning, before I got there. I told them that I had asked Jesus to help me. The church seem to be uplifted after that statement. When I looked around the congregation, I could see it, people appeared to be rejoicing. The whole atmosphere changed; you should have seen it. I could see the pastors getting caught up in the moment also.

Personally; I have never been in such a spiritual space like this in my entire life, It was amazing. I talked about how agnostic and resistant I was. I had become so therapeutic and philisophical over the years with my practice that it some how hindered my spiritual growth. I did not see much use for spiritual guidance. I talked about how witnessing Eugene being saved in the hospital not only changed my way of thinking, it also rearranged my spiritual understanding. I was different by the time we left the hospital, and I was blessed with the Holy Spirit. I told the church that I was convinced I would feel my brother's spirit as long as I stay connected to the Holy Spirit.

I honestly believe that if I keep my temple (my body) right, I will remain in spiritual contact with all my loved ones. I am willing to do everything I have to do to live in the Spirit. When I finally looked around the church, there it was. I knew the Holy Spirit were present and using me as a vessel. For me to be able to even acknowledge such a spiritual concept is a miracle because I have never been at such a spiritual state in my life.

I have experienced a true spiritual awakening, witnessed by many, all praises to the God of my understanding.

This has to be one of the proudest moments of my life, thank you my Father God. On my way back to my seat, I made eye contact with my sister Magary. We were and are very close. If you could have seen the pride in her eyes. I almost melted with gratitude as our eyes met. To have someone I respect and love look at me with such pride and love is truly a blessing.

Magary always loved me like that when I was young I use to visit her and my brother Bobby in Brooklyn. In fact when I look back Ma and Magary were crazy about me they always showed me love. I could remember when our older Brother Dave was killed, Ma seen me coming through the front door of our house, and began screeming my name benji and then she screemed David is dead and held me tight and wouldn't let me go. She knew I was headed down his path and that was her way of protecting me.

My biological mother left me in the hospital when I was born, and Eugene and I were placed in the Nixon family home, a home where we called our foster parents Ma and Dad, and we never referred each other as foster brothers and sisters. It was God's mercy that placed us in such a loving home. Tell me, is our Holy Father great or what?

By this time, the church was flying. I realize it had very little to do with me and all to do with the Holy Spirit; you could feel it through out the church. When I sat down, I was so high and grateful I never wanted to come down. Some of our family members got up and spoke. One of my sisters, who was always a clown, had a few words to say. She was uplifting and amusing. I think the church appreciated her lighthearted humor. Then my younger sister, Lisa, got up her nerve and said some encouraging words about how God was playing a major role in her recovery process, which was a heartfelt message. Our cousin Peanut got up and spoke. I was always close to him, and he talked about how, when he got to the church, he was feeling remorseful, but after listening to my testimony he felt uplifted. That was a blessing, but it was only the beginning. The pastors began to give their sermon. By this time, the church was soaring with the Spirit of God. One pastor after another just talked about how they felt and how blessed they were to be a part of something so glorious and uplifting. A friend of ours and the brother of an old girlfriend of mine, who happens to be a pastor, got up and said he just had to say something. He mentioned that he decided to come at the last minute. He said he was not going to make the trip, and was truly grateful that he did. He actually quoted from scripture, gave his testimony, and then began preaching for a brief moment. Man, we were having church; this was no funeral service.

All you heard from that point on was halleluiah, amen, thank you Jesus, and everyone was joining in.

I cannot describe it; you had to be there to see God moving in this church. All the faces in the church seems to be glowing, while rejoicing, singing, and shouting. It was as if the ceiling of the church opened up and the Holy Spirit just gushed in like the rain and soaked the whole congregation. I could feel this warm, happy, embracing current flowing through the church. If I didn't know any better, I could have sworn the church was suffering from a Holy Ghost hangover. People were just shaking their heads, hugging, crying, and smiling. How can you ever forget a moment like that?

After the service was over, we all went downstairs in the church and were given food and drinks. When we were done, we socialized for a while, and started saying our good-byes. However, before I left, I had something to mention to Pastor Charles.

I told him that I gave my life to Christ, and I accepted Christ as my Lord and savior. He nearly went berserk. Man, he jumped and shouted and kept saying, "Praise the Lord, praise the Lord, praise the Lord." He hugged me and dragged me around to other believers, saying, "Have you heard? Brother Johnson has accepted Jesus Christ as his Lord and savior.

Thank you Father, thank you Jesus, thank you Holy Spirit."

These last two weeks had been the turning point in my life. It was an unforgettable experience, and one that is still having a major impact on my life today. Over the years, I have experienced all types of obstacles, trials, and tribulations that have affected all areas my life. However, through this transformation, I have learned some valuable lessons while getting to know God in a more intimate and personal way. The Holy Spirit has taught me the true value of life and the importance of relationships. I learned that the true wisdom of God comes through the Holy

Spirit, and it takes a certain level of faith in order to obtain it, surrendering to his will is the key.

I approach all relationships with kindness, and if I can help someone I would. I see one God, one Christ, one Spirit, and one Human. I do not put any institution above the love of God or Man.

I am not a perfect man, that is free of sin. Like all others, I fall short of His glory. However, in spite of all my shortcomings, God has blessed me with the precious gift of the Holy Spirit. This was without committing to any type of a religious format. I became willing, open, and submissive to His will. I am that thief on the cross next to Christ who came into faith in a moments notice, and granted mercy through the Holy Spirit. I'm not saying that to minimize the impact of any religious beliefs.

This is only but to show the true majesty of God and the Holy Spirit.

Moreover, with the faith I have in Him, I am capable of recognizing the love He has for all of humanity. I honestly can say although my spiritual fellowship remains inconsistent, I maintain a strong prayer life and a realistic, intimate relationship with God, Christ, and the Holy Spirit.

Through God's love and strength, the Nixon family remains intact. It is only by the grace of God that this story has been written. *HALLELUIAH.*

In loving memory of
Brother Eugene
(Kirk) and Teddy
Thank you Father,
Jesus, & The Holy
Spirit

With Love Talib /Ben Johnson

Dedication

To the beautiful Nixon family who brought me in as a child. That made me feel loved, protected, and wanted.

The decisions I made had nothing to do with the way my mother and father raised me.

I was given a good foundation and structure to live by.

I alone chose the path I took. So I'm dedicating this book to my family: David, Tommy, Magary, Bobby, Phyllis, Valerie, Preston, Debbie, Eugene, Lisa, Vanessa, Celina, Michael, Teddy, and most of all my mother and father, David and Magary Nixon.

Also, a special dedication to my children, Lisa, Allen, Malika, and all the families that touched my life over the years:

The Worthingtons, the Lewises, and most of all, my best friend and wife for fifteen years, Muzette, and the many people who had an impact on my life in Ellenville, Kingston, and Middletown, New York, and Salisbury, Maryland. Hey Rowdy Thanks .

It was the encounters over the years that God has blessed me with that made me who I am. I will be forever grateful. Amen.

8th Love Benji

Surrender to the Spirit of Thy Father

]I am nothing, and only truly something filled with your Holy Spirit. My heavenly Father, I'm starting to realize that I am but a clean slate. I come before you, my Precious Father, not as a black man, a Christian, an American, a addict, a counselor, a father, a lover, or a husband; I am only as you see me. My Father, I am but an infant, for you to apply your will. So I ask you, my Lord and savior, take my will, my life, my emotions, my personality, and

Thou will be done, for I realize that my will is but a rebellious mass of confusion and selfish desire. My will is only to please my flesh and escape ill feelings. To seek out ways to feel good and maintain an emotional high. Father, you know what's best, and your participation in my life is of perfection, because only you can be perfect, I beg that you bless me with that of little attention, for I know that any attention is larger than I can ever imagine, or conceive. So please, my Holy Father, just but look in my direction, and I will be blessed with more Spirit than I can stand. Thank you, my Father, for my faith allows me to know this in which I ask, will be your pleasure to grant. AMEN in the Name of Jesus. Your son, Talib,Ben Johnson

LaVergne, TN USA
02 February 2011
214847LV00001B/7/P